TRANSIENT CITY

a time spent in los angeles

GURDAUR DUHRE

Self-published debut edition, October 2019

 Self-published in the United States and Canada and distributed by Kindle Direct Publishing, a division of Amazon. Originally published in paperback in the United States by Amazon in 2019.

ISBN: 9781088588550

Book designed by Gurdaur Duhrè

Printed in the United States of America

For the city of angels
I hate you, but I love you.

Author's Note

In late August 2018, I boarded a one-way Amtrak train to the city of Los Angeles. I stayed at a hostel on Melrose Avenue, restraining myself to a lobby couch with my antidepressants reacting in my body. I spoke with close to everyone who checked into that popular hostel. I had no other choice than to remain within the vicinity of my stay in case I lost myself. With anxiety, you're not looking for a place to stay, but you also don't like the idea of waiting. You're continually racing with your thoughts, and if you try, the worst of us lose its complexity. My biggest fear was stepping outside or leaving too far off from the hostel itself. I planned to stay, to find some lawyers to assist with my transition to the United States, but that never happened and was unlikely in the current form of politics. With my nerves twisting my gut in the worst way imaginable, I remained on the rooftop on a beach chair soaking in the California sun. During this time, I met a lot of exciting stories from an abundance of travelers. My routine day was often spent on long walks in the morning before any of my dorm mates were awake. The shower was still warm, the provided breakfast untouched and fresh, and subtle noises of hair dryers from the women's dorm was the only loud sound.

I had no intention of releasing these written bits as they were my best medicine until I went back to Canada to get my refills. Stumbling back into this folder labeled with specific events, I understand the therapeutic importance of writing when suffering from mental disorders. Without writing, I would be insane, deceased, and floating without a pulse beneath the chilly waters of the Golden Gate Bridge. My dream is to live and die in California because there is simply no other place like it in the world. The Golden State comes equipped with the best of the ugly for self-discipline. The temptations to divide sinners and romantics, the gravity of chance, and an array of cheap Asian restaurants in little spots scattered across the city and the valley. Today, I am sharing these stories with you because it serves some guidance perspective of a solo traveler. I leave the comfort of Canada to a country that is all but certain and a state far from perfect. Perhaps you, the reader, may refer to this on your solo trip to Los Angeles but I'd like to begin by excusing my cynicism. With time, troubles, and thoughts, this combination of traits can often displease the choices of words on a page. I assure you everything from here on out is the truth through tired eyes. I am not sugar-coating, but writing as my mind delivers. So, without wasting and killing any more trees, I give you Transient City: A Time Spent in Los Angeles. Thank you.

tran•sient - ***adjective***
lasting only for a short time; impermanent.

My Mom

My mom contends against the idea of me going to Los Angeles. These travels have no intent, not a vacation, but merely a walk in the park to hear a new sound, a new street, and talk to faces I've never met before.

"Why don't you stay at home like the rest of them?" She argues. "How come they never abruptly leave to the U.S. as you do?"

"I don't know," I say and leave it to that.

There's an undeniable romance to passing moments. Especially sitting on a train watching landmarks and picturesque motions of landscapes. For a second, you engross yourself in the forest, the street lights, and the strangers waving hello from boardwalks near the abandoned lakes and rivers. And that's it. What more can you do in that? We're paying homage to the second hands of time in a favorable dimension; the window seat of an old fashioned American train.

"You should do something with your life, everyone you know has gone to school and are doing big jobs making a lot of money. What do you do? Write? Has that ever paid the bills? Has it bought you the big house in the hills? No."

I chuckle. My ongoing feeble attempts to persuade me to drop my plans last minute and cancel all my reservations.

"Mom," I get up from the staircase tying my shoes. "Have you forgotten that explorers did not discover this home, this land, and all that it carries with college degrees? Sometimes it's not about the paychecks, moreover, what can you bring back from the unknown."

My mom doesn't respond but walks away. Somewhere she has stored these issues for a future argument when the time is in favor of my little mistakes growing up as an adult.

The tenets of existence since the conception of the universe was neither on paper or written with a pen. It was moving. Action. The inclination to dare and question the stirring fear in our stomachs of living life alone in a new place, at a different time. The right time.

I am in perpetual wonder how much of the world happens at once. All I could feel now are the golden flat plains beyond Albany as we inch closer to the golden state, California.

Something Unpredictable

There comes a time in everyone's life when we begin to fall in love with the simple pleasures in life. Our thrills are no longer Friday night drinks at the bar, climbing mountains, and amusement parks. Our Friday night thrills become the racing heart when your new co-worker you find attractive asks about your day. Our mountains become speaking to those who matter most, and amusement parks become the life we take on with strangers that are now your friends and perhaps even family.

In Los Angeles, you're either poor, or you're rich, and there's nothing you can do to hide either of them. In Vancouver, back in my home city, I've always seen it evident those who conceal their financial weaknesses and those who show off their incredible wealth. This type of divide encourages the silent reserved mannerism of many of the residents.

The ability to know yourself freely, whether being poor or rich in Los Angeles was the reason I learned to breathe through the smoke. People are far likely to judge you here but are quicker to leave a poor man. The emotional attachment is scarce in Los Angeles. The journey of something genuine is only fictional. Who we chose to love here is a trek through rough and raging waters and a plunge that'll either kill you or test your ability to make it out alive.

The soul-searching in the city of angels is the longest and impatient journey you will ever encounter. There are faces, and there are places, and there are dreams we all want for them to intertwine in the magical way a Disney film infatuates us. The truth of this matter is, there is no rest in Los Angeles. Everyone is always waking up to a new world. Like a frog leaping from one lily pad to another. The same way people here move forward with their lives.

I guess if you build a city with a lot more freeways and fast cars, our faith grows deeper into those things than the life around us. All the mid-west dreamers and East Coast hearts ventured to the west coast alone or with others, and they found a universe of stars they can finally call home. At the same time, the addiction to the motions is a lesson to learn. It is not enough to be in a city as vast as Los Angeles and expect it to give you something you desire. You make yourself a needle in a haystack and you either make it out the hay to stitch the fabric of your life, or you get lost deeper and deeper into the golden void and vicariously live through our idols.

It's not where you go that makes a difference in your star-struck dreams, but who you know and how you get to know them. Some lily pads are larger than others but most likely to drown with larger than life egos. The L.A. dream is not a fun one.

The Survivor

My Spotify stream disconnected as I lost all cellular service passing over the Washington Cascades. Our train was at nearly 5000 feet above sea level. My heart pumped blood faster than usual as I peered out the window and saw the vast body of water, the jagged edges of rocks, and the pool of evergreen trees that curtained where the wildlife resides.

I unplugged myself to greet the scenery, and for the first time, I could hear the conversations around me. I listened to the voice of two women seated in front of me on the train. One had a strong British accent, while the other had a grim unwell voice and a terrible fluid-induced cough.

"I would love for Benedict Cumberbatch to cum inside me." The elderly lady replied to a pre-existing conversation I'm glad I had the misfortune of missing. The girl sitting next to her exploded into laughter.

"I'm sorry, I'm just a raunchy old woman."

"Good lord." Said the young girl, "I think that is every girl's dream."

I missed the entire context of the conversation, but I sneered and chortled a bit, but not loud enough for them to notice. I didn't have any part of that conversation.

Later that evening, when people were settling into their coach seat for sleep, the woman got up from her place and locked eyes with me and smiled.

"Oh, where are you coming from you handsome devil?"

I smiled, "Thank you, I'm from Vancouver, Canada."

"Ah, a Canadian. The good guys. How's the summer?"

"Short." I joked.

The woman guffawed, and as the train began to depart, she stumbled. "I'm not good with balance. Especially since my surgery. I lost my left breast from cancer, so now there's this space I'm not used too."

"I'm sorry."

"No don't be. I'm still living now ain't I?"

"Where are you traveling from?" I asked as I removed my laptop from the seat next to mine so she could sit down.

"Lincoln, Nebraska, but I was in Seattle for a month to visit my sister."

"That sounds lovely. Seattle is beautiful."

"It is, I admit. I wish I could have stayed. Sorry, excuse me, but I forgot to introduce myself, my name is Francine."

"Well, it's great to meet you, Francine. I'm Gurdaur."

"Pleasure to meet you too."

I raised my bottle of soda sitting on my table stand. "Here's to another hundred years."

The woman laughed followed by a terrible cough, "God's got jokes giving a lady like me this much hell. And this train, good lord. Have you ridden these through the night?"

"I have, yes."

"Notice how fast they go at night?"

I blank out trying to remember the nights on the Amtrak, and I was sure from experience, yes, these trains do pick up speed middle of the night.

"Straight hauling ass. I'm telling yeah. I cannot stand the speed."

"Is that even legal? You know? For them to go that fast?"

"Oh, of course, if the engineer knows what he’s doing."

"That sounds comforting."

"Just coming down out of the mountains alone we're on a roller coaster ride."

My anxiety began picking up at her words, but at my best of ability, I remained calm.

The British girl returned with a cup of tea and saw us both talking and exchanged a welcoming smile. "I just got my tea, and I feel quite happy right now."

"She hates me." The senior woman replied. "She keeps drinking fluids when she has a bladder of a goldfish. And then she wakes me up while I'm sleeping. Can you believe her?"

"Oh, quiet now." The girl made her way to her seat. "Aren't you lucky. You have an empty seat next to you."

"True, yeah. I had one misfortune of sharing this seat with a man wearing VR Goggles."

"I saw that," The elderly woman replied. "Why was he wearing that thing?"

"Perhaps a video game, or maybe not a fan of the scenic route."

The man we were referring spent a whole three hours wearing those virtual reality goggles. I remember looking at his arrival tag above our seat number and read, 'PDX – Portland' It was only noon, and he hadn't moved. I had to use the restroom, and I hadn't eaten since five in the morning. When I had the opportunity to ask, he places the goggles over his eyes, watching god knows what.

When I couldn't tolerate the wait, I tapped his shoulder, startling him in confusion. He reached for his headphones, then his goggles, then both. I made my way to the small bathroom booths.

It was the first time I caught my reflection in these mirrors. I remember a day, a year ago, sitting inside of these tiny empty stalls learning how to smile after a break-up. I looked into the mirror, convincing myself I was okay.

It worked, partially, because I found the tiny bathrooms quite humorous, but nothing prepared me for what my emotions would do to me mentally when I came back to those haunting four walls of my bedroom.

When it was nightfall, Francine found me sitting alone in the glass car watching the stars as we crossed counties and state lines down the west coast of America. She asked if she could join my table and I nodded a quick yes. I became her outlet for the night to the tempo of the train cars rattling over the aged tracks below us.

"I remember being in the hospital, going through Chemotherapy. For another cancer I had, these treatments that usually consist of 50, I was on 52, and my doctor wanted me to do three more. I told him, doc, you give me three more of these and I'm pushing on daisies. So, he did another scan, and the cancer was gone."

"That's amazing."

"Yeah, it felt like a miracle. But it honestly has made my body so weak I can barely get around. I can't even sit a few hours in a plane hence why I'm on this train. If I mess myself, I can at least have several cars to use the bathroom instead of one dinky one located in the back."

"Fair enough."

"You know what makes me feel very sad."

"What's that?"

"During my treatment, I was the second person with this particular type of cancer. Very treatable. It was rare, however, to have the two of us at the same time. Sadly, the other lady gave up."

"You mean she-…"

"She let cancer kill her. I didn't get it. It was curable. The treatment was hell, but still very durable. Why would she do such a thing? You know?"

"That's rough. God knows."

"Well, I hope so. We all have our time eventually. We became friends, and I thought she was going to live through it with me."

"Oh?"

"She checked out one day and didn't leave me a phone call or a message. She just left. And then a year later one of the nurses told me she had passed away."

At that moment, I thought about our existence as humans. The greatest fear we carry unknowingly is death. We fear it more than we fear to live the wrong life.

But if I was Francine and this was my life, why would I hold on? Even as her body became her enemy, she carries on. Francine rides the train, visits her sister, and goes back to Nebraska until next time. God forbid, but if it ever came to the point in my life with cancer, I wish I have the strength of this woman.

Welcome Back

This hostel doesn't compare to any of the ones I've stayed at in California. But for the sake of privacy, I'm just gonna call it the Hollywood Hostel. If there is a hostel with that same name, it's not that one.

My Uber driver drops me off at the front steps of the building, and I patiently wait for one of the employees to open the door. When the door opens, I see a familiar face. Daisy.

Daisy remembers me from my very first visit back in the summer of 2017. In fact, if you visit this hostel, you might find a picture of me on the wall. That was their thing to make the atmosphere seem a lot homier. Whenever a guest checked out, you would get a polaroid on the wall next to the other thousands of people who have visited.

In the summer of 2017, I was a lost cause. After a fight with my ex-girlfriend, I ventured far away from the valley into the heart of Los Angeles. Daisy was the first to assist followed by Adam, who worked evenings, and the other temporary workers, Rachel and Elizabeth.

"Welcome back!" Daisy opened her arms for a hug. "It's so nice to have you back. Are you here to stay forever, please?"

"I wish," I said. "All in due time. I'm still working on a plan. Not sure when, but I'll know I'll be here soon enough."

Daisy tossed one of my duffle bags around my neck and made up the staircase. The steps were plenty, and for anyone with weak knees, this was definitely not the place to be. The walls inside are painted a warm yellow with wooden flooring and a beautiful chandelier. The lamps in this hostel were something to admire since the owner was also the owner of a lamp shop right next door.

My eyes are drawn to the wall of photos, and I take my time as I pass that first picture of me covered in dust. I wipe my thumb over my face remembering all that led up to that one particular photo. Daisy notices.

"Did you find yourself?"

"I did. It's almost like going back in time."

"Yeah? How so?"

"It's a long story."

"Okay."

After checking in, I made my way up to the roof of the hostel. As anticipated, I see about 2-3 other faces on their cellphones, some sunbathing, and others sharing a cigarette. The strangers smile and wave at my entrance, and I wave back. I step to the ledge of the roof and look down at the sidewalk. I scanned the traffic, and the Hollywood sign soaking in the heatwave on the hills facing north.

"You from here?" One of the guests ask.

I turn over and find a man, shirtless, with tattoos over his rough hairy chest and the side of his arms. He has a cigarette sticking out from the bottom of his mouth and a silver chain around his neck. His body is stretched out on one of the beach chairs with dark tinted shades over his eyes.

"No, sorry, I'm from Canada."

"My name is Elliott. I'm from Casper, Wyoming." Elliott sticks out his hand, and I follow with a handshake.

"Gurdaur, Surrey, Canada."

"Ah, a Canadian. Welcome to America. Cigarette?"

"Thank you, Elliott, but I don't smoke."

"Why is that? Think it's gonna kill you?"

"Maybe."

"You're right, but it doesn't matter to you. You got free health care if you get lung cancer."

"I don't think it works that way."

Elliott doesn't respond, and I'm uncertain whether or not he's asleep now or just ignoring. Regardless, I count cars below before I hear Elliott snoring with his cigarette bud pierced into an empty tin can of beer.

Where Is My Daughter?

The next morning after breakfast, I'm sitting meekly at the usual lobby couch chair charging my cell phone and scrolling through the map of Los Angeles drawing out my day. Daisy, the hostel staff, is taking the morning shift and answering phone calls of upcoming reservations.

I've meant to go to some places I haven't gone in the past. I'm probing the hidden corners of Los Angeles opposed to the tourist hotbeds. My main attraction, however, is coffee shops with cute names. Ten minutes later, the hostel doorbell rings, and Daisy sluggishly makes her way downstairs.

"And so, my day begins." She groans.

When the door opens, I hear a disruption. A wailing. "May I come in? Please. This girl is my daughter." The mother sobs. I can hear her coughing and choking on her words.

The conversation is hard to hear with the passing cars and traffic in the background. I try to listen carefully, but I can't make out the words.

"I'm not trying to say we won't find your daughter. We are. Come inside." Daisy responds, assuredly.

I greet the paramedics swiftly while walking to the bathroom. The mother standing by their side is wearing an elegant blue coat like something out of a fashion magazine, and she's rubbing her eyes in distraught and smudging her mascara.

A group of heavy footsteps is approaching the upper level of the hostel. Daisy looks at me with a look of suffering and mumbles, "Drama, drama, and more drama."

I look closely at the paramedic's clipboard. I see a name that begins with the letter N, but that's all I can make from the writing.

"When did you last see her?" The paramedic asks.

"Not too long ago. Noel had breakfast and talked to me for a while. She's perfectly fine."

"But she is my daughter. Last time she went outside on her own she walked into heavy traffic. I don't want that happening again to my baby. I need you to see that this is my daughter."

"Mam' I want to help you. Don't think I don't want you not to find your daughter. I do."

A woman, a much older voice speaking Korean, comes up the staircase. She's on the phone talking a chopped and stuttering English.

"Mrs. Farlow?"

"Yes, that's me."

"Here, it is your daughter."

I see the Korean lady, possibly the owner of the hostel furious at Daisy as if it's her problem. The exchange is subtle, but I read the fear in her eyes and the rage in the owner.

"What seems to be the problem?" The owner asks the paramedic.

"That's a private and personal matter. You don't need to worry about it."

"Yes, but this is my hostel."

"Stop! Please. I need to talk to my daughter." The mother shouts. I get up from my seat and move towards the men dorm to give respect and privacy to this matter.

"I need you all to stop. This girl is my baby. She's not a crazy person. She's sad, upset, and wants help, okay. She can know. My daughter is living here. So please, stop."

The paramedic laments and looks to her partner. The two exchange a look of weariness acknowledging the awkwardness of communicating with the mother and the people around us.

"She always does this to me. I don't want her to kill herself." The mother cries. "I'm trying my best to give her help, but she lashes out at me."

I walk to my dorm and hear the loud gravelly voice of the anxious mother and the somber tone of the paramedics. I move away from the door and see that everyone has left the hostel to enjoy the picturesque weather outside.

I lift the flap of curtains in my dorm and look at the smog choking the blue sky. The cars below pass one behind another. All I see is the calamity of walking in the middle of the chaos.

Chances of survival are low. I wonder about this girl in this city and what makes her chase defeat in this dry, unforgiving and boisterous traffic. Her reasons might be the same as mine, but then if she did kill herself today in the blistering sun, was the day not enough or is the beauty of a clear day as disposable as the romance we can never find in Los Angeles?

The Yogi

"I sense some deep energy from you." A woman tells me from behind as I sit on the bar stool on a counter. I was in the kitchen writing and catching up on leaving a review for a recent stay at an Airbnb. She coughs heavily as If she has a cold. I try to retain distance from catching her cold.

"Sorry?"

"See, I'm a Yogi, and I read people's energy all the time, and there's something about you that I feel is so powerful."

"I appreciate that, thank you."

"I'm Dana."

"Nice to meet you, Dana, I'm Gurdaur."

We shake hands. Dana is a spiritual lady. She has all these necklaces around her neck and exceptional jewelry on her fingers. Dana looks to be older, perhaps in her fifties. Her dark hair is neatly tied into a small turban, and in her hand, she's holding a Rasta shoulder purse.

"You're not like the rest are you," Dana says. "You're not following the crowd, I mean. I see you're just sitting inside in a city like Los Angeles, but you're not from here."

"It's a shame, I know. I've been outside. Just not the places I don't feel I need to be, however."

"You're young, I'm guessing 24."

"Correct."

"From Los Angeles?"

"No, I'm from Vancouver, Canada."

"Oh, but you're, like, you're Muslim?"

"No, I'm Sikh, Indian descent."

"Right, I understand. I saw you. And I mean no offense, but I saw you're of a background harboring a great spiritual tradition. I go to this Yoga place every morning, and we do this special Yoga specifically for Yogi's like myself, as you can probably tell. People think I'm crazy, but, that's their opinion."

Dana was a fast speaker. I smiled endlessly taking no offense to her words, her approach, and what she had to tell me. Continuously she coughed. Later, Dana told me it was the hostel, making her feel congested than usual. I was relieved as I was attempting my best of ability to not fall ill on a long-term trip as this one.

"So, do you have a lot of friends here in Los Angeles?" Dana asked.

"A small group of friends. Yes. I see them as much as I can. They've been people to me in my life and the only reason I can learn to love this city as much as I do. Not in that infatuation with Hollywood Boulevard touristy type but little things, you know? Also, with a touch of hate, we all find in our own home. I don't think you can truly love a place all the time. I love The Winchell's Donut House, the laundromat, the parade of vehicles on the 405, just the motion of this city and how it grows the people."

"This energy. You're walking with everyone but not physically. It's like you're seeing the world and the people they meet, their actions, regrets. You sense it all. This explains why you're not outside."

I'm a bit flabbergasted at her words. In an odd unknown way, she was right. This was precisely how I felt. The world was happening outside. I knew that, but sometimes I felt the people around me. Regardless of strangers or friends, there was a path I wanted to know, to be part of and understand.

"Yeah, that's a divine perspective on it, I never put it into words like that before."

"It's a total Yogi thing, I'm sorry if this is coming to you a bit of a shock."

"No, I appreciate it. It's comforting."

In the background, a group of hostel friends and other solo travelers linger. Dana observed them and told me how amazed she was with the younger generation and how despite the turbulence of the growing and chaotic world, we seemed to play it calm, docile and going on about with our lives as the problems never existed.

Perhaps that's our survival instinct. Instead of fighting the negative energy, we ignore it in somewhat of a self-destructive way. We connect with other humans, other people we deem worthy of our time in our own filtration system. It's a river of the unknown we swim through trying to find the time, people, and the essence of respect that can be shared in a harmonious pattern. A simple gesture but most likely to always fail in moment's notice.

People have an idea of Los Angeles, but honestly, it's a vacuum. There are the lights, sounds, the people. The youth curse and cuss their friends and streets. To the outsider, we think of it as glamorous portrayed by the pop stars of America, but in reality, it is a home with new palm trees, warm weather, smog, and insane drivers. As for the stars, I am sure that if you can't find them in the skies of Los Angeles, you're bound to find them on the ground. It has always been that way, but most of the time, nobody is really looking.

The Daughter

The next morning around 5, I'm first to wander the empty chambers of the hostel. Los Angeles is waking up in sounds of trucks, cars, and the grouchy homeless man spitting and vomiting around the corner.

A few hours later, Daisy enters the dining room setting the place for breakfast. I make my way down and bring my notebook to sketch ideas for an upcoming novel. I list of characters, plots, events, and every other detail I will end up removing in the final draft.

"Good morning, Daisy."

"Oh, Gurdaur. I didn't see you. Look at you, you're all dressed up for a minimalistic photoshoot in Los Angeles."

I laugh as she describes my all-black attire and my hair for the first time in a week, wax, and pulled back. I feel refreshed, especially having the time to shave.

"What are your plans for today?"

"Not sure, maybe reload my bus pass for the month."

"Sounds thrilling."

"I woke up bright and early just for that."

Daisy smirked, pouring a glass of orange juice for herself and collecting a plate of toast, donuts, and strawberries.

After breakfast, I got dressed to get my bus pass reloaded. At the same time, my anxiety began peaking. I could feel my heart rate increasing perhaps from the coffee. I had gone coffee free for a month seeing if it would calm my nerves, but in reality, had done the complete opposite. I sat down, attempting to breathe.

A young girl in her pajamas walks by, I smile to give her my greeting, but she stares at me blankly without expression and walks to the front desk urgently.

"What did my mom say?" She asks Daisy, who is sitting at the front desk running errands and check-ins on her computer.

"She was just very concerned about your well-being."

"I told her not to come here."

"She is your mom, Noel."

"She's a burden."

Noel and Daisy speak quietly together. I can tell Daisy is trying to assure her that everyone means well to her safety. I connect the dot, and her face shows a resemblance of her mother.

I remove my gaze and go downstairs to the dining room and lounge. I grab a plastic cup to get water. Noel comes downstairs and looks at me again, and once again I smile, and yet she doesn't smile back. Her expression and her mind are elsewhere. She isn't at the hostel. Noel's thinking about things, but still, I don't know who she is, where she's going. I want to talk to her, but I don't know what to say.

Landon

A week was almost gone, and I hadn't made any escape from the hostel. My medication was running low, and I was far from getting my refill in Canada. I had to make wise choices.

A set of footsteps came sprinting down the stairwell, and that's when I met Landon. A springy young man from Atlanta, Georgia. Blonde short hair and his attire of white, red plaid shirt, khakis close to that of a young man going fishing with his papa.

"What's happening everyone?" He greeted. "It's so quiet down here, why not go outside?"

I didn't speak of my issues but nor did anyone else. My reason would send off a red flag, but my personality didn't like an awkward silence. For an entrance like this one, I had to speak.

"Still deciding."

"Oh, that's fine. I'm Landon by the way."

"Nice to meet you, Landon, Gurdaur."

"What are you doing out here?"

"Good question. Still trying to figure that out. How about you?"

"To be frank, this is my pre-wedding getaway."

"Just by yourself? Where's your wife?"

"I'll have a lifetime to take her around everywhere. This is just for me."

I shrugged, "Fair enough, but how old are you exactly?"

"21 years young."

I wanted to comment on his age and his plans to be wedded but who was I to critique. People of my culture marry at a much younger age. My own grandmother from my mom's side got married at the age of 13.

"Congratulations."

"Thank you."

Landon wasn't the regular guest. He was moving his hands a lot when he spoke of his passion. His goal is to become well known in Los Angeles for something noteworthy. Not particularly the arts and not for a scientific breakthrough. Something more.

"We can't waste this time!" Landon said halfway through his motivational speech spree. "We're in the city of stars, and we're sitting here. We should go outside and make some videos, film something, make a lot of big movies!"

"You're all about it, I like that," I said. "Let me know how I can help."

"Do you have a camera?"

"I do."

"We're already halfway there."

Landon tapped me on my shoulder and waved me to come upstairs. The other guests still were disinterested, but this was my time in the city, and my meds were working, so I knew I could handle Landon, whatever he wanted to do.

The Girl I Left Behind

I once loved a girl nearby from this city, and when we broke up, I never felt more like a needle in a haystack.

Los Angeles is like the universe. It's the city of angels and stars. Except all the stars are stuck in big houses in Calabasas glued onto the hot black tarmac.

I'm not a California native. I was born and raised in a city less populated than in Los Angeles. My hometown is a bedroom community. Men, women, children, mostly from overseas, come to my town of Surrey, Canada. Surrey is a close-knitted environment until each square block is what many consider, *"Little India."*

However, the title of this book is Transient City, and many might argue every city is a transient city, but nothing tops Los Angeles. Compared to the closest town to me, Vancouver, Canada. We hold a small population of 700,000, but Los Angeles is built up with nearly 4 million according to the 2016 consensus reports.

Los Angeles is a transient city by formation. Never stopping for anyone who wants to be there with a definition. The city of Surrey and Vancouver is quiet. On the grand scale of things, nobody matters in Los Angeles. If you lose friends, nobody comes back to reconnect, if someone breaks your heart, that's it.

It'd be foolish not to think you're not replaceable in a city with over 4 million people. The moment you find anything you love in Los Angeles, you're just as close to losing it, forever.

With such vast differences in our populations, I've always felt growing up that there was still time to get something back in B.C, time to enjoy something, get something back, and maybe some of us in this province are not as replaceable because it's all just trees here. When things end in my city, we go back to what we know because if it isn't that, it's only trees. Hills and hills of trees, mountains, wildlife, and Tim Hortons.

My friend says she admires that of Los Angeles and I tell her there's a certain romance to a fleeting moment. If emotions in Los Angeles had an analogy with an intimated object, it would be the coaster of the drinks served at the local bar.

You wish everyone would use one, but half of the time it's fallen on the floor or not even used at all. Los Angeles isn't heartless. It just doesn't care about you the way you wish it would care.

Everything and anything of you comes from the basis of your surface, so if you want to be recognized, noticed, and feel like you matter, you will either go crazy before you get seen or be noticed for going crazy.

Charles Bukowski

In my mid roaring twenties, I wander inside a bar, I order a drink that I won't drink, and people are all around me. Some older, some younger, and some the same age as me.

"Hey?" A young woman in a violet dress sits next to me in the booth, "Is this seat taken? But I'm just waiting for a friend, that's all. In case you know."

"No. Please, there's no name on a bar stool."

She's drinking from her glass full of bubbles and condensation. Her laughter is contagious and silently attractive like a Venus Fly Trap. The bar is one aisle at the grocery store that has everything on your grocery list. When you walk inside you're either looking to wallow your sadness in toxic fluids, Band-Aid the pain from ex-lovers, or self-validating if people still find you attractive. I'm not going home with her tonight, I think. Should I let her know? She's pretty, but for once I don't feel like thinking with my dick. I let her go.

I don't like Charles Bukowski. I love writing, and he's probably a half-decent guy who had a whole lot of hardships, but when I read his poems when I see his face, I want to throw up. The vile honesty always made me feel like he glorified the worst of people when they're vulnerable.

I don't tell people I'm a writer. I say to them I'm an editor, I lie. Somedays I'm the Washington Post, and some days I'm the New York Times, but regardless of the answer, the girl who asks is still wondering if I find her attractive.

I give her another drink, and I buy myself another. I slide both glasses to her. She's in ecstasy. Her girlfriends, loud, hysterical, and deuced with perfume surround me. All the while I'm hoping the last two glasses were enough for her to filter me out and go for that douche bag in his white polo shirt, greasy hair, and with a name like Tim, Jeff, or even a name with three or four other names. I don't feel terrible. In this city, there's another her down the block at another bar.

It's two in the morning when I return to my hostel, and it seems most of my roommates are in the lounge watching Netflix. I can hear the laughter. One of the guys is explaining the movie with an intensity that it's ruining the entire film altogether. I locate one of the water boilers and make myself some ginger tea. The scent of alcohol is sticking inside my nostril, and I'm feeling sick.

"What are you watching?" I ask without a formal greeting.

"Captain Philip"

The guy continues rambling about the film. A few of the girls from the dorms are scrolling on their phones disinterested in the synopsis. I sip the herbal tea squinting as the spices tickle the back of my throat.

When I go back upstairs to my room, I already see some of the backpackers asleep, a few of them are on their phones, and one guy is openly clipping his nails without a napkin or paper below his feet. I can only imagine what he's thinking, "It's not my job." Fucking disgusting.

My bunk is close to the window. I picked it specifically to hear the noises, the smell, the drunks, the prostitutes, and the faint sizzling of the food truck cooking food near the gas station.

I dreamed a lot about this city when I was just a teenager. I drew that Hollywood sign in all my school notebooks. I made goals, aspirations, and dreams. When I look at that sign today on top of the upper floor balcony hostel near Sunset Boulevard, I wonder how much somebody gets paid to clean the lettering, surveillance that sign, that eight-letter word that makes people around the world think being here will make them the next big thing.

We don't become everything we believed, but we get halfway enough to sip it, touch it, and overwhelm ourselves in temporary highs to boost our confidence and self-esteem.

Being a famous nobody in Los Angeles is a lifestyle, but as long as you're there, somebody who isn't here still finds you unique as another famous person.

Lily, and the Sun

Maybe it's this Sun. When I think about my city and the abundance of inclement weather, I wonder how much of it decides our emotions.

When it rains, we stay inside. The passenger's in the city buses in Vancouver always frown, snobbish, or seem like they're about to erupt into an angry seethe about life.

There's an acrid taste in my mouth as I wake up from under my bedsheets. I cough nastily for a few seconds. My chest feels full huffing the horrid odors coming from the window that's been open all night long. I don't sleep too well, it's five in the morning, and the guy on the upper bunk bed is snoring hazardously loud. I stoop my legs over the side of my bed as it makes a loud creaking noise and possibly waking up some of the people in the room.

"Sorry," I murmur to myself as I glide on my shoes and make my way to the bathroom.

I see the hostel maid running her first chores. She's mopping the lounge, sponging down the bathrooms, clearing the showers all before the morning rush.

"Morning, Lily." I smile in my bleary and exhausted voice.

"Oh, morning." Lily greets, a bit startled to see me awake before the rest of the guests at the hostel.

Lily is Chinese. She speaks English through a noticeable accent but doesn't occupy in many conversations. I've met Lily on several accounts during my stays at this hostel, and her work ethic remains the same. When Lily was my age, she was in the army. Today she is most likely the same age as my mom, perhaps her early fifties.

This visit was my third trip in my life where I made reservations at this hostel, and her cleaning service was impeccable. There was never a single crease on the bedsheets, and the question of her technique led me to discover this was her life at one point.

She would wake up at the command of her leaders. They'd clean their living area to the core, leaving no smudge, no stain, and of course, no crease in the bedsheets.

"Nobody knows." Lily tells me sometime last year, "I escaped. I didn't like the army."

Lily is one of the many immigrants who migrate to the U.S. to escape unforgiving living conditions in their hometown. Sacrificing family, friends, and even tradition. When Lily isn't working, she smokes cigarettes near a lamp shop. I see her on the phone, but she doesn't text or call anyone. Lily reads the news from China and hardly shows regard to the manic noise of Los Angeles.

Before breakfast, I take a slow walk to a small bridge that overlooks a freeway. On several accounts, I contemplate jumping for the sake of knowing something I don't want to know. I hardly think like that anymore. Now, all I think about over this bridge are the blank faces in behind the cars.

When their great-great distant grandparents arrived in this city, they the promise was the American Dream, and most of them got that, but nobody suspected their future generations would despise everything it would turn out to be. In many ways, I feel birth is selfish greed by two who thrive for the achievement of a lifetime, however, have no regards the problems their children onwards will face. It's all for the moment's satisfaction.

Parents feel guilty telling their kids Santa Clause isn't real, but aren't as guilty when they realize their children will suffer from never genuinely aspiring to be anything more substantial than life.

I give my greeting to a group of people, one of them turns to me asking for the Hollywood/Western Metro Line station, and I point straight ahead, "It's at the four ways straight ahead, near the Starbucks."

My sunglasses are in my pocket, and I feel the warmth of the Sun getting closer to my skin with every passing minute. I guess today the weather's going to be great, but I'm sure nobody will talk about it the way they do in Vancouver. A clear sky is nothing new in Los Angeles.

The Japanese Lawyer

For the remainder of my afternoon, I made myself comfortable at the table located in the lounge to work. My hostel mate, Jeff, a retired wrestler, and coach had recently been accepted into programming directing job in Los Angeles. However, Jeff is from Wisconsin, and his booking was only for a week.

"I need to compromise," Jeff said aloud. "I can't go back to Wisconsin."

"It's just milk and snow in Wisconsin." I said.

Jeff chuckled but remained in distress, pulling his hair between phone calls, requesting, begging, for his friends to let him crash on a couch. Like most people, Jeff had fallen in love with the L.A. scene almost upon arrival. Today marks day one for the rest of his life as he got accepted for the job of his dream.

"Hey!" An elderly woman exclaimed walking into the lounge. "This free computer?" She asked.

She was in a bathrobe and had an accent. She left her purse on the counter as she sat down but later remembered to pick it back up.

"Yes, it's free."

"Oh, thank you."

The first thing this woman did was put on Japanese music on the speaker. The second thing she did was go on her phone and laugh. Eventually, she left altogether, leaving the foreign Japanese music as ambient to the whole lounge.

"Why you in L.A.?" The woman asked.

"Soul searching."

"You look for a girl? Marry?"

"Yes, I'm looking for at least three." I teased. "Can you help me?"

"I can do it. I am a lawyer okay. Very true."

"I don't doubt it."

Jeff overheard our conversation and the aggressive tone of this lady. Neither of us knew who she was personally as she might have checked in within the next half hour.

"You live or work in America?"

"Sorry, mam, I'm from Canada. Vancouver."

"Do you want to live in L.A.?"

"Maybe. Someday. If I have a lot of money. If my books ever sell."

"No, you need a green card. American green card."

"Can I get them at Walmart? Or 7/11?"

She caught the joke this time and almost hit me with her purse. I grinned. "I'm sorry. This is why I'm hardly the biggest fish in the sea."

"Fish in the sea? Why? You looking for a woman or fish?"

"Are you interested?"

She cursed in Japanese. "You have charm. Perfect charm. But you're skinny. You need to be stronger."

"Darn, I knew I was missing something."

"When you get married to an American girl, call me."

"Do you know any single American girls?"

"I'm a lawyer! I know many!"

"Really? Are you a dating lawyer?"

"No, no, I work at Japanese Consultant in Indianapolis. People do it all the time."

"Isn't that marriage fraud?"

The Japanese lady smiled at me for a long time, "Are you gay?"

Jeff blurted out in laughter. I kept my poise. "No, I'm straight."

"Then?"

For a lawyer, she was demanding. Almost like a strict teacher or a mother. She wanted me to find some sort of order and way to naturalize into America.

"I guess I should go find me a decent woman."

"Pay me a membership fee. I will find a good girl."

"How much?"

"Two thousand dollars."

"I'll settle for one hundred."

"What is one hundred? Here? One hundred is nothing. Ha. Don't fool me. You silly."

I never got her name, but for the sake of this story, I'm going to name her the Japanese Lawyer. Jeff had left the conversation as we got more into deep-rooted discussions about politics.

She adores Vice President, Mike Pence. On her phone, she had pictures of herself and Pence at a Christmas dinner. He had a grin. I scrolled through a few more photos and saw more photos around the Christmas tree and then at a fishing trip somewhere perhaps in the mid-west.

"Pence, a strong man. Trump not so much."

"You're Republican?"

"Yes, proudly. I come from Japan to Hawaii, and now in America. Very nice people."

Moments before I could add onto her words, the lawyer pulled out her wallet from her robe pocket and openly began counting hundred dollar bills. Jeff kept his glance leveled with mine. When she wasn't looking, we shrugged uncertainly to why she was counting this money openly without fear.

When night had fallen, I sat upstairs on the same couch I sat on before. This time she joined me on the seat without asking me to scoot over.

"So, where is she?" The lawyer asked.

"I'm telling you, the offer still stands. It could be you."

The lawyer pushed my face away with her hand and went back to her room. Noel was coming out of her hostel dorm and witnessed the departure.

"What was that about?"

"That's me making friends with the people of the hostel."

Noel shook her head and went to the bathroom, scratching her hair and yawning. I wish it could be Noel. The more I heard her silence, the more I fell into that emptiness. I could listen to her laughter even when she wasn't there, and I knew this well I fell into was getting deeper.

The lawyer came back and smiled when she saw me smiling, "What, who was she? Is she the girl?"

"Say it any louder?"

"Was that the girl?" The lawyer said a pitch higher.

"God, help me."

"Oh, finally. An American girl for you."

But Noel isn't American, she's Brazilian. Trying to find her place in America. Walking the hot tarmacs alone, scrubbing toilets, doing a job where she can't build the castles she wants to build. If I knew a way for her, I would make it for her. However, there is a lock on her door, and I often knock when we lock a smile, a conversation or unknowingly feel close to one another even when we're not in the same room together.

Western and Lexington

Somewhere around Western and Lexington near a bridge that looks over a freeway is a giant sign that warns residents to get tested for HIV. I look at the sign that shows a woman smiling on the poster. In the corner, it indicates she's a specific patient at this office. Her name is clearly shown.

It's a rusty neighborhood. Garbage, clutter, and construction are happening not too far from where I'm walking. A mother and a child walk hand in hand while they talk to each other in Spanish. I regret not taking up another language. I always tell myself to practice Spanish before traveling to America. I embarrass myself frequently.

My fear runs dry on these streets, but others would tell me to be careful. My attire is relatively new, I have my wallet on me, but when I walk by the sketchy faces, they don't look at me. In this world, we all have an agenda. Whether we're piss broke or filthy rich. We're going places, but we're nowhere close to happy. Not for a long time, though.

At the Dark End of the Street

Wandering this city has led me to see temporary highs in a momentum faster than the second hand of a clock. People wait for the bus as I finish loading up my tap card for the month. The Metro Red line passes, and I realize the stops are nowhere close to me. If they were, I'd skip the smaller stops brought from the Orange Line. In the end, I continue walking.

My anxiety is fading, gently. My stomach settles into hunger. I recall a lot of my time in the city thinking about the life of an American born and raised in Los Angeles. As the years move forward, nothing is far from cheap. People will do anything to have a dollar. The patriotic American has put too much faith in a failing leader. His people eat with laughter, while cities, counties, and states below watch and wonder, collecting crumbs; "What did we do to deserve this?"

My late-night walk around ten at night departing from Cal State, Northridge. I've been in contact with Cal State Northridge in the past for post-secondary education. At this time of the night, it scarcely has souls in and out of the campus. I remember these streets vividly during the day. In my mind, I think about the ridiculous debt manifesting most of these students. A mortgage a lot of them will pass-on and perhaps take to their graves.

I come to the first street light around the campus and find an ad posting of minimum effort printed in black and white requesting, "Cam Girls, Escorts, and Nude Models" The ad is vague for it speaks for itself and guarantees young girls a payout of a thousand dollars or more weekly. All but a few tabs have been picked off the contact sheet. On it is a Gmail, a name of Ryan, and his phone number. I turn around hearing a conversation of a few students departing. I continue on my way into the night.

The American Dream for most Los Angeles hearts is a desperate one. Behind these many college apartments and windows rest the troubling mind of young men and women being swallowed from the system. An education system that accommodates people a debt, an education, a degree, and the unforgiving reminder that all that glitters is not gold.

I accept this is the reality many of these faces have to deal with, and I am in no position to judge, but observe. My tender heart of thirteen years old dreamed of a life similar to one only seen on television. However, the more I walk down these streets, alleys, and all the corners you don't see on Ellen, Jimmy Kimmel, and in Hollywood. I realize the ladder for anyone not leveling the eight-letter sign is a long one, even if you are born and raised in Los Angeles.

Sakura, The New Girl

Climbing up the stairs, I listened to the voices in the hostel. I saw some new faces, some old. Rachel, one of the girls who began working at the hostel, was sitting in front of her computer. I greeted her, and her face bloomed with a beautiful smile.

In my dorm was another story, it involved a man, his fourth Corona and my friend Landon from Georgia who'd fallen ill over the last few hours.

"Men are just chaos on a stick." The drunk man announced. "All we have are dicks, we think with it, we're always horny, and if it ain't that, we're hungry."

Landon and I looked at one another trying our best not to laugh. I looked over to his bunk, and intently heard him preach cynical wisdom about a woman. Above his bed read the name, William.

"William."

"I don't like that name, but that's what it is, William."

"I'm G."

"Nice to meet you, G. In case you want to know what happened, this is what happened."

William, a man with long hair and even a more massive beard, passed me his phone while drinking down a bottle of Corona. "Women will fuck you up."

The contact ID above the messages read, Sakura. I had met Sakura earlier today when Rachel was juggling three guests at the front. The doorbell rang, and she was out of breath.

"Do you want me to get that for you?" I asked Rachel. Rachel smiled forgivingly.

"That'd be great. Thank you so much."

I walked downstairs and opened the door. A young girl, perhaps in her early twenties stood wearing a red tank top and black shorts. On top, she had black shades and light brown hair nicely put into a ponytail with a red bow. Sakura looked like a school-girl, but the real allure came when she took off her glasses and revealed the Earth-tone eyes and the sprinkle of freckles over her nose.

I helped her with her luggage, and she introduced herself as Sakura. A half Japanese and Kiwi *(New Zealander)* Sakura had been working a few summer camps and been traveling around the U.S. Los Angeles marked the last leg of her travel before she'd head home to the Oceanic continent.

William had gotten to know her, in fact, he obtained her number and abruptly began drunk texting her minutes after. The texts ranged from requesting to hang out and empty greetings. And now, William drank bottle after bottle spitting his heart out. Landon lay shirtless on his back listening while I leaned against my bunk bed gathering in his words and thoughts.

"Women are so lucky." William began. "They have the looks. They're all beautiful. Even the ones that aren't can be beautiful, so in the end, they're beautiful."

William continued ranting about Sakura and how his ex-girlfriend reminded him of her. "Dude, we met, and within two days we fucked every other hour. And this was a year ago."

The thoughts weren't linear. The way William spoke jumped from one mental strain to another. At one point, he began talking about Instagram and how everyone has Instagram, but he only has nine photos and one follower, which was that every girl he had sex with a year ago.

"It's easy stuff, you can go up to a girl and ask for her Instagram, and they'll give it to you because they want attention. Guys don't have that selling factor, you know? We're just as we are and we look like shit. We have a god damn organ poking out of us all the time whereas girls got curves like cursives on a Coca-Cola font. It's all a marketing scheme to get young people to drink their sodas, but you know what I mean?"

Long after William departed the room to apparently attend open-mic, Landon looked at me with a look that asked the same question I was wondering: "What the fuck just happened?"

"Thank God you're here. He's been talking for hours and hours now."

"So, what happened?"

"He tried hitting on this girl, Sakura, and apparently she rejected him silently sending him into a miserable mess of recalling ex-lovers and what have you."

"I'm sorry you had to endure that."

"Dude, I don't know what the hell happened, but I'm sick as fuck."

"How'd this happen?"

"I don't know, I was perfectly fine this morning and then bam, I'm just like sneezing and coughing."

"Something is going around. Elizabeth, the girl at the front desk, was sick earlier too."

"Yeah, well, I don't know. It fucking sucks. By the way, I extended my trip up until Tuesday now."

"That's amazing man, how's the wife?"

"You know, she's fine. But I have to be honest with you."

"What's that?"

"I miss going out, and you know, flirting."

I felt the momentum of his voice lessen at the topic he began talking about. At some point, I asked if he ever had thoughts about infidelity, especially after he got married. However, Landon was straight forward and expressed his life growing up.

"I never did the whole dating and going out thing when I was younger. I wasn't even trying. Being a devoted Christian, I was told everything I ever did was a sin. I can't lie. I looked at girls, I felt things the Bible says I shouldn't feel. And now I'm here, In Los

Angeles, and I want to talk to a girl, but I don't mean wrong to my wife in any way."

"You just want to talk to women, is that what you're getting at?"

"Yeah, like, the same way you talk to Noel or the girls at the front desk. It's not flirting, but you make them laugh, and you're able to get them involved easily in a conversation and then get everyone else involved too."

"I appreciate the compliment."

"It's not like I want to have sex with these women, I just want to flirt a little bit, maybe go out for a drink and dance. I missed not having that opportunity. And to be honest, my wife and I don't even have sex that frequently."

"Oh?"

"Yeah! But I still love her to bits, it's that I'm just a man with urges and I'm hardly able to act on them let alone with her so what else am I left to do? Of course, I'll watch porn or masturbate but shit, it makes me feel like a disgusting person."

Landon's experience in Los Angeles brought him a new world. His eyes opened to the vast land of opportunity, not just work but even in relationships. Experiencing Los Angeles in the mind of a fleeting traveler is tempting. The ability to stretch yourself to being someone else is manageable and exciting. At the same time, it is a disease. It infects you in confusion. Ultimately, you are no longer the roots of your own home. You make up a new one, a new name, a new personality. The escapism becomes a way of life

I Might Be Leaving

For most of my day, I made myself comfortable on the chair located near the front desk of the hostel service desk. Rachel, the staff, talks about her move from Maine and how she's settling into this great big city for the first time in her life.

It isn't too long when Noel is heard downstairs coming up. I anticipate her blank stare, and expectedly, I receive just that but then a smile, a questionable one at most. Almost as if she's always asking herself why she's smiling for when nothing is alright. I don't know if being a part of her life in this small distant way is changing her. I don't know if her mother worries much about her now than she did earlier this week when I arrived in Los Angeles.

Her friend, Eva, is carrying a mobile phone asking to take pictures. Throughout the evening they can be heard creating a ruckus among the staircases of the hostel.

"I don't know what you want me to do," Noel says, trying her best to being a photographer.

"Make it look comfortable."

"Make it look like nobody is taking the picture."

Eva, another cleaning staff, the model of the night, laughed at the comment, and continued posing.

"I'm not a good photographer." Noel criticized herself and gave the phone back.

Noel does this thing where she holds off on smiling unless she sees it first. When she sees a smile, she does two takes, one to make sure it's for her and then again to smile back if she's sure.

"Hello Gurdaur, Hello Rachel," Noel waves.

"She is the worst photographer," Eva says jokingly.

"Hey, I'm good at everything, just not technology."

"She won't even have Instagram."

Eva is a bit of the hype woman school girl. There is always a grin on her face that says she enjoys life, the company, and having any fun possible between folding sheets, doing laundry, and maintaining the hostel. She originally comes from Africa but grew up for some part of her life in America. The two, Noel and Eva stand side by side like loving, playful, and eccentric sisters.

"I'm craving donuts." Rachel burst. "I don't know why."

Eva fixed her white tie hanging loosely over her tucked in a blue dress shirt. "Donuts? At this time?"

"Why not?" Rachel responded.

Noel had left out the door, and a part of me got concerned. Neither Rachel or Eva had taken note on her departure, but I could feel the fear. I recalled Noel's mother sobbing in the center. Apart of me wanted to run out to find her. I don't want her to know what I know about her. I resist. My anxiety is peaking, but I believe and pray she's not doing anything to end her life.

Fifteen-minute later, the door opens, and the conversation has died down. The footsteps are slow and subtle.

"Guess what I have?" Noel's voice peaks out from the staircase and eventually, her face surfaces. In her arms is a box of donuts from Winchell's. Rachel's jaw drops, and she's in disbelief.

"I was just joking."

"Are you still joking?" Noel teases. "Here, you get first dibs."

"Wait, did you bring this for all of us?"

"Yes!"

A few of the guests in the waiting area pick up a donut treat. Noel offers me a bite, but due to my gluten allergy, I have to refuse.

"I wish I can make this better for you," Noel says. "This seems sad for you not being able to eat the donuts."

"It's okay. I used to work at a donut shop. I've had a fair bit of donuts in my life."

"I used to work at a donut shop too. It was called the Donut Man."

"Where was this?"

"South Carolina. I'm going back pretty soon."

I was a bit saddened hearing this, but this would be good for Noel as she mentioned it was going to make her close to her family. I asked for her number, and she said she didn't have her own phone and it was merely an emergency device.

"This one time I asked for a girl's phone number, she gave me her email address. It didn't even work."

"That's hilarious."

"She had a history of giving her dad's phone number instead of her own. Interesting conversations they had."

Noel gave a look of eureka, and her face lightened up. There was a burst of real laughter. Eyes full of tears and cheeks pink beyond the lightly tanned skin.

"I wonder how my dad would react."

"Don't give her ideas," Eva replied.

"Maybe you should test it on me."

"Maybe."

Throughout the night the donuts were exchanged, we smiled, and one point I took a picture of her. Noel rested her back against the yellow walls of the hostel and ate a glazed chocolate donut.

Around 11:30, everyone had gone to bed except for me. I made my way upstairs to the roof. I surveyed the Hollywood sign as I had repeatedly been doing in the past. The sky was overcast, and the air was as chilly as Vancouver, Canada.

"Sleep," I told myself as my heart raced in anxiety. But neither my heart or my mind listened, and I stared into the distance hoping the sun would rise or hoping I wouldn't have to wake up tomorrow to face the same health problems as I was tonight.

Goodnight, Malcolm

I had just gotten back from writing at a small coffee shop fifteen minutes out of the city. In some ways, I did feel attacked from the rainbow text that read, "B-Twenty-Four" I told myself, "I am, I'm trying to be." The UBER driver made a brief conversation about the pleasantness of the new tarmac above a bridge. For the remainder of the ride, he was on his phone, calling, and chatting loudly to another friend or family member in Chinese.

A new reality sunk in much later when I had finally sat down on a couch at the hostel. On Twitter, the name Malcolm was trending, and so was Mac Miller. To my own knowledge, I knew Mac Miller had released a successful studio album. There's been an abundance of promotions for his record on billboards in and around Los Angeles. Personally, his music inspired me a lot to make instrumentals and beats from my bedroom during my teen years.

A few scrolls, and a few clicks later, I had realized something terrible had happened. Mac Miller was dead. I froze. Elizabeth was at the front desk on her phone, and the first thing I said to her was, "Mac Miller is dead." Elizabeth's face was just to close as mine in disbelief. It didn't seem real. I didn't want it to be real, but it was, and once again, Hollywood consumed another soul to its pleasure.

I cannot judge his life, his reasoning, but like many fans and listeners, we wonder what it was that went through his mind during the final moments of his life. Is it a success? The music? Financial problems? A broken heart? Maybe everything all at once. But this wasn't a suicide. This was accidental.

In his own words, Malcolm had spoken about his life in the 2016 documentary, "Stopped Making Excuses" and said: *"I'd rather be the corny white rapper than the drugged-out mess that can't even get out of his house. Overdosing is just not cool. There's no legendary romance. You don't go down in history because you overdosed. You just die."*

Friday, September 7, 2018, for most of us, was just a day on the calendar. In this day, we had our own plans. Mine was at a coffee shop, Noel was sweeping, Elizabeth checked-in guests and the other faces of the hostel made conversation over cigarettes and coffee. For Malcolm, it was an average day too. Perhaps it was another day at the studio, a little rehearsal before the tour. We unwind in our ways, we know our limits, and we live within it.

In this life, we escape more than once in a day. Most of us look into the glass lens of our phones to avoid, some of us run miles and miles until we sweat our guts out. Humans run a marathon to the end, and the race is not an easy one.

Was this the Hollywood people tell us to fear? Is this the abyss that we're warned about when the grass turns a little greener on our side? Growing up, I could convince myself that I would never become that person who loses it all in the hot minute of success and wealth, but nobody loses it from that, they lose it from life. The gnawing chapter that never finishes. The routine agitation of trying to achieve and be stable.

I didn't drink ever. My curiosity had loomed desirably over drinking on most occasions, but if people knew why I would do it, they wouldn't let me at a house party or a night out at a bar. Inevitably, I knew the rush of destruction. Attacking the human container. Attempting to freeing the soul enduring an endless amount of torture and agony from heightened existence. That side of me peaks ever so rarely, and when I find my outlet, I am not gentle. I rage like a hurricane, sweat a monsoon and tremble in anxiety-like the earthquakes in California.

Noel is never leaving my mind. I know once I leave this city, and after she goes to South Carolina, I will worry about her like a mother worries about her daughter. It is fearful to know she does not see what I see when I look at her. When Noel sees her reflection, she hears her stories of hurt, and they talk to her, judge her, and eat her consciousness to sorrow. When I see Noel, I see the complete opposite. But that's what she wants the world to see. To never know the truth about her.

But there are moments in a day when the fragile at heart and the weary of eyes do let go, and it makes me wonder a question I don't want an answer for, but I know she is always seeking, and that is "When? When do I leave?" I hope Noel never finds out that answer.

From what is my fear to a loving girl at a hostel was the same fear someone had about Malcolm. It is unimaginable what this person or people feel today. In constant questioning and outlining, they wonder what they could have done three months ago, a week ago, or a few hours ago, so he wasn't at home but maybe on the phone a little longer, at the mall a little longer or even at a radio station a little bit longer. For those minutes and seconds could have made the difference between life or death. We often don't realize this until it is too late.

Wishful Thinking

Undoubtingly, she's the prettiest girl in the hostel. Sakura. I spent the morning conversing with a group of hostel friends. Landon lit up a joint, the drunk guy William still awkwardly made his advances and failed. Then there was Marcus, a man from Brazil who enjoyed taking pictures of people and using Google Translate to communicate.

"He is not speaking English, he's speaking marijuana," Marcus said.

Sakura chuckled, "Oh, that's a crack up."

"Crackup" was another way of her saying something was funny. She said between anything that sounded funny. Especially the story about William's drunk night in the city.

"So here I am walking down Melrose and all of a sudden a pedo-van screeches to the sidewalk. A man hops out, and I'm like fuck, I'm about to get stabbed. No. Two men, one American and one Russian approach me and ask, "Hey, brother, do you want to buy some TVs? Like a fucking TV. It's two in the morning, so I ask, how much, the American says 2,000, and then the Russian says 200. I almost shit myself."

"Oh gosh, crack up for real."

My mind ever since coming to Los Angeles had been drowning in the ecstasy of women and sweet-talking my way to their front doors. I felt vile, disgusting, a person I didn't want to be. At times, I contemplated suicide. I hated my eyes for looking at women in the lustful way I did. I hated the way I spoke to them with confidence and charm. I hate what I was doing to myself in the process. This is the writer's self-destruction, Da Vinci's broken ear, and his hurtful cry for help wanting for the world to understand his story.

Sakura paused in my words with her sharp brown lit eyes. The islander genes were dominating her smile, and a limited sparkle in her eyes even aided the drunk blind man, William. I said everything a woman despised from a man only to find out Sakura found a youthful and securing comfort in my words. I admitted to my laziness, my anxiety, my lack of will to leave this hostel and enjoy the gorgeous sun in Los Angeles.

When she starred at me a little longer, talked to me a little longer, and I took the word on an open indirect I aimed to be her date for the afternoon, all the while, I had met another girl a few days prior who was expecting me to show up today on our formal date. This meant I was seeing two women at a different time on the same day with the same emotions.

In my mind, I made a wish. An indecisive desire. I wished somebody would break plans. I asked out Sakura, who agreed. I would take her to Venice, take a lot of pictures for her, and then return home and visit Diana, a generous, kind woman I had met online earlier this week.

"Come outside when you're ready, oh, and bring a USB," I texted.

"I gotcha!" Sakura replied.

My hand slipped, hitting the heart emoji, and instead of apologizing, I let it sit there. I made it part of my wave. The waves had taken me to different people and places. Some would consider me a great friend, but to myself, I am my own enemy and somebody I wish I could erase completely to never be seen again.

So, I stood outside for five minutes, ten minutes, and then twenty minutes. The universe heard me, and this was it, Sakura was the disconnection. Eventually, Landon and Jeff joined my waiting game. But instead of waiting, we spoke. It got hotter, and none of us stuck around. Landon went to go attend a comedy gig his Los Angeles friend was hosting, Jeff finished his laundry and inside Sakura was inside with the Japanese Lawyer who was carefully teaching her how to write Japanese.

I pretended as I had come from my own errands and grabbed a cup of water to sit down. I took out my phone, even though nobody texted and eventually spoke with Sakura.

"Hey, I might just chill for a bit," Sakura replied. "Just because like, it's my last two days and all."

"That's fine. If you change your mind, let me know. I'll be upstairs."

I had already felt from her gesture and body language she was going to leave on her own terms without having me around. I don't know how I read that, but I think it was the wish I had asked the universe and now it gave me an answer. It hurt, a bit. There were these sudden smiles and glances much earlier. Compared to Noel, Sakura's smile surfaced much longer upon questioning the stunning expression on her gorgeous face.

"Why are you smiling?" I had asked an hour earlier.

"I don't know." She replied, not hesitating to look away. At that point, I knew I had an obligation to pursue and curate a pathway of getting to know her, perhaps on a different level. It was selfish of me and childish. William's drunk bantering and inexcusable comments had her skin crawling to leave. I just happened to be that one guy. A somewhat attractive, lanky, guy that seems well put together but honestly faces the ongoing battle of social anxiety and the constant urge to consume narcotics for the sake of sleeping forever.

When I see my reflection in the mirror, I like that face, I like the person I see, but when I see myself, it's not my eyes, my nose or my touch. I live almost through the world itself and how it wants to see me and everyone is happy. I smile only because it looks incredible, but deep down, I hate myself for not trying to be myself because I know that person wouldn't be traveling. He'd be at home, on a couch, under layers of sheets and taking pills from a plastic container with seven boxes labeled for the week.

For the longest time, I had an urge to cry. The muscles in my esophagus would contract, and I'd have a difficult time breathing. This began back in July as I worked as a ride operator in the city of Vancouver. I overlooked those mornings of terrible anxiety. I guess I never found something I might lose in such a long time. There was a girl. She was a story I worked on, I wrote in my life but never in words. It always seemed to me that a girl I put in words would be the one I'd have to let go and move forward. I walked away, but there were smiles. A lot of them, and sometimes if I thought about them for long enough, I got through my shifts. However, this disease in my brain is not a battle that settles. It still runs inside me ruthlessly. It tries to overtake my choices. I have no control, and I fear somedays it will win.

The universe heard me again because my other date canceled and even the next few I had written on my calendar texted saying they had errands to attend. I smiled, I breathed and knew that this was something I had put on myself from the very beginning. I've always believed in the words from the novel, "The Alchemist" that when you want something, all the universe conspires for it to happen. It did happen.

There was an abundance of clichés I could think of when the cancelations came one after another.

One of which was being careful what you wish for because if you wish hard and long about it, or even for a quick second, it'll happen. This was entirely my fault.

I accepted this sorrowful defeat by taking out my bag of Oreos from a purchase I made a few days prior. I made myself comfortable on the chair and began writing because between the world outside and writing, there are nothing and nobody that can cancel on the plans I make for myself.

My Anxiety

My body shakes uncontrollably, and my jaw is chattering in either cold or anxiety. I wake up feeling nauseated and anticipating to throw up. I don't, yet my body shakes like an earthquake, and I am ever so stressed than before.

I abruptly get over the side of my bed and quickly put on my socks, grab my medical cards, water, toothbrush, and toothpaste. I sit in the bathroom, holding my face talking to myself. The walls seem brighter, and I can feel my face slowly losing color.

"Stop," I tell myself. "This is all in your head." But this doesn't work. My heart is still racing, and I try to gag but I can't.

"Lord, help me," I say quietly. I brush my teeth, hoping this would relieve my mind of its focus and draw the anxiety away. It works for a while, but my body is still suffering from what feels like a mild seizure.

Outside of the bathroom, I see Adam. He's sifting through some papers and sees me and notices something is wrong.

"Hey man, you alright?"

"No, not really."

"What's up?"

"My body's just acting up, I'm pretty sure it's my anxiety."

"Are you cold?"

"Yeah, and no. It's a bit of both, I just need to relax is all."

"Do you need any medicine?"

"What you got?"

"Let me check."

Adam goes into the staff room and comes out with two bottles. One of them anti-nausea pills, and another is for migraines. I grab the anti-nausea medicines. "Thank you."

I pause between words, and Adam stares at me anticipating the worst. I lower my head and nod assuring I'm okay. One of my thoughts during my anxiety attack was, 'I am here, alone. I know nobody. If you go to the hospital. If you die tonight, you will put your family in debt. Don't do this yet.'"

"I got it from here," I reply with a shaky breath.

"Well, alright, man. Let me know if you need to go to the hospital."

"Won't be necessary. I just need to walk her off."

"Who?"

"Anxiety."

I go downstairs in just my socks, shirt, and jacket. I hold my shoes and put them on without doing the laces. I grab my old Ginger-Aid tea bag and fill a cup with hot water, and another with cold. I take a few sips in the room before I get antsy from the design and feel like the walls are projecting moments and times in my past that I have failed. I leave.

The rooftop is accessible, so I walk onto the few steps to the upper level and grab a chair. I turn on my iPhone and put a playlist on Spotify on repeat. I rest the phone on my armrest with the volume on high. The songs are all designed to aid anxiety attacks. The first song that plays is "Don't Panic" by Coldplay.

The guitar subtly exits the speaker and into my ears. All of a sudden, my heart begins to come to a rest. Chris softly sings,

"Bones sinking like stones. All that we fought for,
Homes, places we've grown. All of us are done for."

The words score the city that I look over. The sky is purple with light but diminishing in smog. The air is struggling. A slight breeze rushes across my face, and I think for a second, if I can see that breeze, I would chase it because it felt good and just like many good things, they end, they move away. To another person, another place. I am not so special to have it all.

A see cyclists below, an odd character freely doing turns in the open roads. The occasional car or two passes below loud blaring music. In the night sky, I try to find the birds but I can't. I'm worried I'll never find the birds and my heart will never sleep, but then I see the cars, the ones that drive slow, drive fast, and I think of the people. Each and every one of them doing what makes them happy. Whether it's working in the shadows of the city or never-ending yesterday affairs of platitude joy; whatever by definition that stands for Los Angeles.

"We live in a beautiful world."

Chris sings on the chorus, repeatedly, and I finally rest. I break down. I am lonesome, I am blissful, and I am tearful. I want to yell at this city at the top of my lungs for never listening, for never waiting, for never believing enough to become something than aged homes, unpaved roads, and settling for the 405. And yet, I am happy not for myself, but for them, because they found themselves in a place that makes their time bearable. For a second, I live vicariously through that world and my heart is slowing down. The only light dimly lighting the patio ignites at four in the morning.

I know somewhere out on the Hollywood Hills, the sign sits waiting for the daily rush of tourists and photographers. Moments later, lights blink and I see buildings I never saw before wake up. I give myself a laugh behind the tears. I must have startled them, I think. The cup of tea in my hand has gone cold but I don't want to put it down because it's giving me comfort. My heart monitor indicates I have reached a resting rate and I am okay.

"I'm okay." I tell myself. And sometimes it's hard to believe those two words but when I do, I still want to cry because for once I believe myself. I feel humiliated even in the darkness of Los Angeles from the tears. I wipe them off and sit back looking at the sky still hardly breaking stars or another breeze.

The thing I realize all at once is I'm not well put together. The books I write does not make me special. My tattoos will never make me feel stronger and the needles that make them will never replace the pain I know. After countless visits to this city, I understand that standing in Los Angeles won't help me find my dreams. I am not the poster child for anything. My love is tremendous for everything and everyone, and yet, measurable. Breaking down is my strength, but finding out the reasons why is my weakness. And when I can't breathe and it's 3 in the morning, my heart races and I am reminded just how fast this world is spinning.

William

The next couple of nights, my sleep was better. Landon borrowed my camera a lot to film with a local aspiring film director living in Westwood. Jeff was working his new job. And William was having an episode of his own.

I was happy with myself for not needing any of my Ativan to help me sleep, but last night, something was not right.

The lights were out, and although there is no curfew at this hostel, it was just common courtesy to not storm in around 3 in the morning and trash your dorm out of rage.

My bunk bed was closest to the door and had William gone any crazier than he did last night, I may have had to use that escape to my advantage.

The evening prior, I was texting Sakura briefly. We were making plans to hang out, but I passed out unknowingly. Everything after that is almost a blur.

I recall the light turning on blinding me and everyone else.

"Turn that shit off!" A man yelled from one of the bunk beds in the back. I personally hid my face into my bed sheet and plugged in some headphone listening to a piano playlist on Spotify.

I heard William yelling, but my dreams were too loud for my mind to even bother to comprehend what was going on. It wasn't until the next morning where I'd learn the reality of William and why he wasn't in his bunk bed the following day.

This is Awkward

In my ridiculous drifting mind of both fatigue and questions, I turn on my phone and send one message out to Sakura. The dorm room lights are all out. It is pitch dark, and the air conditioning is blasting cold air my direction. I ask if she is awake, and she replies she is, however, my heart thinks different. I tell myself I am in a disposable city, I am replaceable, and most of all, I am not the all dying center of the universe here to play some local God. I'm tired, I'm human, and for once I liked myself for not trying because I'm done trying especially when the walls have been built. I went to sleep, but not as long as I wanted too.

As usual, I always saw the odd few people lingering around the halls and staircase. Through tired eyes, I don't see much, but I do see William pushing down his luggage. I try paying him attention, but he looks at me through his dark sunglasses and groans in anger. I continue to the bathroom without any real regard.

On the rooftop of Melrose Hill, I see the gray smog, the humidity, and the muckiness settling into the world. It's near six and traffic is calm for the most part. I look at the palm trees, and the Hollywood sign faintly making its presence on the hill across from me. I think of all the hikers, tourists, and the photos people take to this sign.

The moment I see flying birds, I stop and stare at them. My anxiety peaked a bit in the shower, perhaps from too much of comfort. The birds help me remind a faster and rapid motion. It distracts me and fills me with a kind of hope as if one day, I too will fly that high and look down at Los Angeles in interest. For now, I stand on the rooftop, looking at the heights I struggle to reach. It is me, my build, my universal genetics, and the unknowing path before me. I keep walking waiting for the day I fall into a sinkhole and arrive in a new city.

I pace around the fake grass on the roof level. As I make my way around two chairs side by side, I discover a ring. This particular ring was not usual. It had sort of a door hinge dynamic to help with the flexing of a finger. In fact, it looked more-so as two rings attached together. I know who this belongs too. The father, Elliott. The East Coast native who was abandoned by his wife, who took his child pre-birth and has been refused to see his daughter for two years.

Elliott had been trying to reconnect with his wife. However, he told me she wasn't right in the head and made false accusations and misrepresentations of abuse. Doing things like calling her sister, swerving the car and hitting herself to blame him.

And now, in Los Angeles, Elliott is on a pursuit to work on his music and create art. Landon had been involved deeply into the conversations of art as Los Angeles is all business for him. Comparatively, Jeff had a job in Northridge now letting him escape the dreadful winters of Wisconsin. And for myself, I was still the writer sitting in the corner hearing ex-husbands, crazy lawyers, and a crack addicts find their way in life.

I placed the ring in my pocket along with brass knuckles that were on the ground. I figured they belong to Elliott. In some ways, he was disgruntled with his life and losses. He spoke calmly to others and perhaps had a winning attitude.

When I re-entered the men's dorm close to breakfast, I saw Landon awake, but William and Elliott weren't at their beds.

"Hey, see Elliott around?"

"No, but hey, look who left?" Landon pointed at William's bed, which lay bare with no bedsheets.

"Checked out, already?" I asked

"Dude, that guy was not right in the head."

"What happened?"

"Just last night, I was up on the roof, and he just began saying how he doesn't like people shitting on his philosophy. Then he was like, 'I know what you're doing. It's cute.' And we were just talking about our lives in general, but then he began talking about people taking advantage of him and pursuing hidden agendas and stuff like that. He argued and sort of left."

"That's weird, perhaps he was drunk. I heard something but slept right through it all."

"Maybe."

Breakfast was far from ready, so I made my way back to the roof with Landon.

"I'll catch you upstairs."

"No worries."

It wasn't until moments after he arrived when his face was in shock. "Sakura and Elliott hooked up."

A bit of me wasn't surprised as Elliott was the far off one and an older man in general. Sakura, still eighteen going on nineteen with a young heart and curiosity to match and also, both of them were in transit from their own cities and own places.

"How'd you figure that?"

"Downstairs, man. Elliott and Sakura are cuddling naked."

"That's awkward. Are the guests having breakfast around them while they're cuddling?"

"I'm not gonna lie, something happened." Landon raised his eyebrows. "I thought he'd be serious for his music, but his intentions really show at the moment. He's not here to find his dreams at all. He's running away from his problems by being a shitty person."

"Explains why I didn't see him last night."

"He just picked his stuff up and ran off at one point in the night. His belt is on the floor, and so is everything else. I thought William and him got into a fight, but no, I guess he had other plans."

This was Los Angeles, I figured, and William fell in love. Falling in love in this city almost seemed sacrilegious. The amount of ecstasy in the air and lust was not built to permit the idealistic Hollywood romance, it was the complete opposite. When you visit a city so vast and scary, emotions are all vulnerable, and the conversations are short. There's no time for mind-games, just simple, pleasurable, self-redeeming games.

When I walked down the staircase towards the men's dorm, I saw Elliott and Sakura both standing face to face in their pajamas. Sakura had a tired look of hesitance while Elliott carried on the suave appearance trying to persuade her of something. "Morning," I said and back, they bid me a good morning too.

My pre-cup of tea that morning was the Japanese Lawyer who took me by the arm forcefully and said, "Hey, that girl, Saki, Saku something."

"You mean, Sakura?"

"Yes, she is a bad girl. She is a hooker. A prostitute."

"Why do you say that?"

"She on the roof with tattoo face and they do fuck."

"So?"

"Do you like her?"

"I'm not judging her."

"You do like her."

"At least I don't judge her like you."

"She is a bad girl. I show her photo to tattoo face, and then they fuck upstairs."

I got up from my seat and proceeded to another table. The woman tried to get my attention much further, but I really didn't need her toxicity infiltrating my muffins and Ginger Tea. I put my hands in my pocket and felt the ring and brass knuckles. I had yet to give them back to Elliott. Gradually, everything connected on how it got off his hands the first place and why most of his belongings were scattered on the bed.

For poor William, this was heartbreaking. He came across as someone who confused cynicism for wisdom and most times washed down his words with beer.

His sober heart still longed for a girl that once gave him the time of day to matter and feel important, but what he never learned was to move on carefully and find a new meaning for his life than dwelling on the old.

Of course, in some distant and unknowing way, I had caught some feelings for this girl, but they vanished when I realized that a smile just means it's a smile, and if it's just for a little longer, you are still not the most important person in the world.

I, we and everyone else is replaceable, disposable, and one thing doesn't change that, no, not even a shoulder punch. Unless the person makes it knowingly distinct, perhaps in words or written text, everything is a game, a test of ego, and willfulness to match the cards together and pursue the urges humans so often dwell upon.

Romantic films told us that the first guy and the first girl we see in the movie are bound to fall into inseparable love. What we forgot was it was all a movie, and in real life, the first girl and the first guy in the two-mile radius aren't going to be your lifelong sweetheart. They'll just be a face you'll put away with other thoughts. A stranger. Another reason for you to be cynical, recite drunk philosophy and abruptly leave your hostel at five in the morning when you see your crush fucking another guy.

The Quiet Goodbye

In the pageant of life, she was misunderstood. I saw a lot of myself in Noel. Every time Noel would frown even in the happiest of settings, it was because she knew something she didn't want to know. That happiness is never permanent. It's running away, escaping like that feeling of getting a new toy for Christmas but losing all of its joy and pleasure by the following year.

In my own twisted imagination, I liked to think I was able to make some difference in her life. As if the moment I first met Noel, I wrapped a rope around her waist and one against mine. Whenever she wanted to jump or run into traffic, I pulled her back and gave a second chance. My only scale to measure that were the times I was able to make her laugh and make Noel forget, even for a second, that the worst things in her life were drifting clouds detaching and fading into the rain to the city below.

Maybe running away for her was more manageable at this point and for the better. I knew Noel said she was going back to South Carolina but whatever she was looking for here wasn't down there or in New York, Paris, and every other beautiful city.

These things take time because happiness can't be sought until it is found inside our busy hearts. Not from another soul, but in our own routines. In my time, I was still learning to discover that away from my pills and shortcomings.

I felt like Van Goh's best paintings that he never got the chance to paint. I wanted somebody to believe I was going to be okay and if I were the canvas and Vincent was the artist that everyone should take his words when he says, "I'm going to create the best work of my life, it'll take a lot of pain, but It'll be my first and last."

In Los Angeles, I learned you're never complete, but you never let the city know. We are all incomplete in the city of angels. How we find that full circle is by dipping our feet into the vibrancy of the nightlife, pictures, and contributing a strand of our hair to the arts calling it fame and fortune. We are all sinners, we are all dancers, painters, and actors in Los Angeles, but our only audience is our bathroom mirror.

The hostel was sound asleep except I was on the leather couch next to the single golden light of a lamp. I had a mug in my hand with cold water listening to the sound of rain on my cellphone. It was around 3 in the morning when Noel came downstairs carrying a suitcase in her hands and tears in her eyes.

"Hey," Noel said.

"Are you leaving?" I asked.

"Yeah, I just need some water."

"That's okay."

Noel's mind was made up. The suitcase was zipped up, and she had cried herself dry for days, months, and maybe years. The rope around our waists was cut, and she was running where her heart desired.

She wasn't going back to South Carolina. Noel was going somewhere further than that to find herself, and I understand that feeling dearly. When she finished drinking her water, she threw the cup in the trash and walked up to me.

"Noel?" I stood up to assist with her luggage but instead her arms wrapped around me into a long firm hug.

I stood, stunned. In a wave of warmth, this was precisely what we both needed this time around. We had demons we befriended but can't tell us between friends or foe. It was our demons that were hugging, not our pure souls. "You're going to be okay," I said.

Noel sobbed, and I could feel the warmth of her tears soaking through to the skin of my shoulder. She looked at me with no words but smiled leaving me a broken rope but granted a key that if in this universe we ever cross paths, I am more than welcome to walk inside her heart and be friends again. That was enough, and like that she left the front door of the hostel never to be seen again.

Van Goh

Landon and Jeff were downstairs in the kitchen. Today was there checkout day. They were happy, but deep down, I knew they wanted to stay much like everyone else who came from a small community.

"I'm going to come back, I just know it!" Landon said. "I can't stay in Atlanta. This is my place."

"Bring your wife next time, maybe she might like it."

Landon laughed and made a face disagreeing and that possibility. Jeff, on the other hand, was frustrated he hadn't saved enough money to support himself for another month.

"If only I had another grand, I could have made it work for me here."

"You learn something every time you come here. At least that's how it feels to me."

"Yeah."

"Next time, make that extra thousand, come back and find that old job and make it work. It's all here. Los Angeles isn't going anywhere."

Landon knocked against the wooden floor, "You never know, this place gets a lot more earthquakes than anywhere else."

For me, it was upsetting to see Jeff and Landon depart. Their stories were different, and their motivation was real. Somedays I wish I could find that trail that led me to this city back in 2015 and do everything a little differently. It was my eagerness to see this godforsaken city that made me happy, broke me terribly, and made me realize this is a place I could call home.

In my definition, you call home a place where you can build a mountain, break it down, repair it, and learn to love the journey in between. Despite all the errors, the missing portraits, rejections, and breakups, we are that lost Van Goh painting. Infinite bliss is fiction, and happy endings are only in Hollywood films. Life is far more than that script and priceless to be sold to the sun. And yet we wonder, we drift and think just maybe the best of Hollywood is watching us from afar ready to throw us some slack in the form of fortune, hot cars, and first-class tickets, but it won't. It never will.

Laundry, Pizza, and Chill

Later in the evening, Sakura had come back to the hostel with a group of guys and girls. I was in the middle of a conversation with Daisy when Sakura approached the counter.

"Hey, excuse me, sorry, do either of you know where I can get my laundry done?"

"Yes, this dashing young man can help you with that seeing how it is his third time here."

"I guess I do have laundry to do, let's go."

"You're not busy, are you?" Sakura asked

"Not at all. He's just saving me from these dreadful long hours at work." Daisy sighed. "You two go get your laundry done. Don't worry about me."

I grabbed a duffle bag of my laundry, and she came out with a duffle bag twice the size.

"Wow."

"It's all from Miami and New York," Sakura replied with a smirk. "It's gross, I know. I should be more prepared, but I was such in a hurry traveling and whatnot."

"It's fine. We can just combine our load since mine is like less than a quarter of yours."

At the laundromat, we took a seat after disposing our dirty laundry into the machine.

"You game?" I asked walking towards a flashing arcade screen for Super Street Fighter 2.

"Is that a challenge?" Sakura asked.

"If you want it to be, sure."

I'm not Sakura's type, and Sakura is a type of girl I might never have a chance with but it was then I could look at her without the die-hard need to impress. Sakura was a friend, and I was okay with that.

"So what happened between you and Elliott?"

"Can we not talk about that, please."

"Okay."

Sakura tried to focus on the arcade game, but I kept taking her character down in a one on one wrestling match.

"It's on my mind, so we have to talk about it." Sakura fessed. "I didn't know he had a family."

"That's the kicker for sure." I teased. "I saw you two that morning at the doorway in a close conversation. What was that about?"

"He just got really weird. He wanted me to move in with him, marry him, and stuff like that. It was just too much, and he wouldn't stop texting and following me."

"You really had him wrapped around your fingers."

"He was just a fling, that was all."

"Hopefully that didn't ruin your stay."

"No, it was cool. I met a lot of cool people here. I mean, I think you're the most chill person I've met at this hostel thus far."

"I'm flattered. I think you're the worst."

Sakura was defeated in the game, and her eyes were on me in disappointment, "You don't really mean that, do you?"

"You're such a crack up." I laughed.

"Fuck off."

"I got you good, though, right?"

Sakura ignored and playfully nudged me to the side.

After we did our laundry, we went for pizza. Sakura got pineapple and ham, and I got a plain cheese. Sakura wasn't acting the way she did earlier around everyone else, and then I thought it could be an age thing.

At some point, everybody wants to be something they can prove to another in a discussion. The person who has done A, B and C. Opposed to the person fearful of doing the daring and courageous.

"What's next for you?" I asked Sakura.

"I don't know. I know I'll do this again next year, but I really just don't want to work for the rest of my life."

"I feel that."

"I want to live here someday, but I don't know how that's going to happen."

"Why do you want to live here?"

"Just a lot more to do on this side of the world. Don't get me wrong, New Zealand is beautiful, but I want a change. A big change."

It's not the worst Sakura loved about this city but how she was able to make the best out of the worst on her own. When you come out of a place where the risk between life and death are little to none, it's easy to fall into a stage of procrastination. When you're in America, your entire life is fight or flight. We're all embracing our rags to riches story one shitty day job at a time.

Without daytime television, the happy faces of Kelly and Regis, the entertainment from SNL, Late Night hosts, and Ellen, Los Angeles would feel like a third world country.

Many residents would agree, The U.S.A has slowly fallen behind next to the other nations in this world, but all those other nations going a little further ahead saw the possibilities of how great the United States could be if it wasn't insane for most of the time.

And maybe that insanity is what people like Sakura and I fall in love with. The extreme culture, the unknown tomorrow, and the possibility we might just make the best damn thing this city has ever seen in its existence. Landon saw this city far greater than his own, Jeff hesitated to even depart, and I had a hard time knowing what the people here wanted from me when I made myself known.

I've learned to abandon formality in Los Angeles and to just pick a drift and ride with it to where it takes me. When I come back to Canada, I step into the shoes and feel like a soldier waking up at a certain time, wearing clean wardrobe and attending to my prescribed duties in a wholesome manner.

Los Angeles was waiting and even if we were sitting in a dingy corner store having the sloppiest wet pizza as you would expect, we were creating a hope in our heart that would never die as we would get older and closer to our deathbeds. We would all be back but not together and all that matters is we make it to that destination at some point. Not as winners and not as losers, but as ourselves, gentle and fierce as we become.

All The Places We Never Went

As my days wind down to the last three days, I have noticed how the faces that check into this hostel remind me a lot of those in Vancouver, Canada. They look at you, but they don't smile. Last night I spent my evening from 7:00 PM and onwards in bed, writing, listening to people check-in and check out. My usual position on the chair was left empty. I have nothing more to feel at this point. Even in general passing, all I hear are the mundane conversations, and most aren't even in English.

Sometimes I think about those places where my former love and I never got to go. Los Angeles is a crowded but lonely city for me. The absolution I desired was simply a fragment of an idea, it may have started out from a kid under a palm tree who saw the stars, the nice cars, and the beautiful faces. From there he walked behind them, hoping maybe someday somebody would find him and take him to the places where all the happy people go.

He worked a little longer, thought he had found love once, but lost it twice. Worked around his feelings and eventually he was no longer that kid under the palm tree, but an old man watering his dying garden in Glendale as his sidewalks got more occupied with white hybrid Toyota Priuses.

We ate at cafes we couldn't afford, walked along the Pacific Coast Highway to Malibu. In my memory, all those days flicker in the agitation of film strips of rusted mute colors, but every day, I lose a piece of it from my memory until finally, I bare nothing else of that time except the mere notion something beautiful once happened.

We got sand beneath our toes and a lot of it in the car. But when the seasons faded and we no longer went to beaches, the sand dried up and the grains still linger beneath the glove compartment. No matter how much we vacuumed and tried cleaning it out, somewhere deep inside the fabrics rests those minutes and seconds we hurriedly got in to go home and love the best way we knew how.

I am not that wise old man, but someday I will be old. Whether I'll be wise or not is not what I thrive for, I just hope someday I can look less at this world and look at my own. I have experienced life in a way I hope nobody dreams of discovering. Every step that wasn't my own, I was there maybe one step too many ahead and learning a million more behind them trying to get forward.

The life of a writer in my eyes is not a simple one. We're not always here. Some nights, I have learned, in the ways my father didn't is to put down the things we hold close to our egos.

For him were liquor bottles, his mundane job, and his money he wasted on those things to make his ego, and for me, the keyboard beneath my finger and the pen in my hand. It became abundantly clear to me as a young writer that began writing out of despair and desolation that when we get all that we once thought was fiction, we're ill-prepared, taken aback, because something inside is telling us: *"This wasn't supposed to happen."*

I revisit those old places on my own now. I walked across Los Angeles like a cemetery filled with gravestones with every epitaph reading some of my favorite memories and now even the worst ones. As I bury that time next to what made me smile, I have learned to smile for the loudest and lowest points in my life because eventually, everything makes me all that I am today.

Gurdaur Duhrè was born in Surrey, British Columbia Canada but spent most of his time writing in and around Los Angeles, California. He is not a New York Times best-selling author. Gurdaur does not come from a family of talented and wealthy artists. Nor was his parent's doctor's, lawyers, and every other succession of admirable, inspiring occupations that would make an otherwise professional writer seem credible. Duhrè began writing through poverty at the young age of 5 on the backside of flyers and by recycling paper. He moved a lot in his childhood and by the time he turned 18, he packed his bag and embarked on solo travels down the coastline from Seattle to San Diego. Gurdaur doesn't have a blog for you to cite his 'award-winning' writing. He believes owning a domain and having that much free time would ultimately make him broke, behind on rent, and unable to feed himself and his family. In 2018, Gurdaur released his debut novel, "A Sudden Grey Sky" on Amazon and a poignant honest compilation of journal entries from a time spent in Los Angeles in 2019 titled, "Transient City."

Made in the USA
Middletown, DE
16 January 2021

31864298R00061